DREW SHENEMAN

HARPER

An Imprint of HarperCollinsPublishers

AUTHOR'S NOTE:

This book is based on the work of thousands of scientists and researchers who dedicated their lives to digging through rock and dirt to unravel the history of life on Earth.

In 1863, anatomist Thomas Henry Huxley first suggested the link between dinosaurs and birds, but the fossil record was small and the evidence elusive. Back then, the prevailing wisdom was that dinosaurs were simple-minded, lumbering beasts. Groundbreaking work by paleontologists, like Yale University's John Ostrom in the 1960s, has revolutionized our understanding of avian and nonavian dinosaurs from the plodding, cold-blooded reptiles of the past to the dynamic, diverse creatures we know today.

All it took was a hundred and fifty years of tireless research to figure out that birds aren't just related to dinosaurs, birds are dinosaurs!

For Don and Kate, because why not?
—Drew

Reviewed by Dr. Luis M. Chiappe, Gretchen Augustyn Director at the

Dinosaur Institute of the Natural History Museum of Los Angeles County.

Library of Congress Control Number: 2019946117
ISBN 978-0-06-297234-7

Design by Drew Sheneman and Chelsea C. Donaldson
20 21 22 23 24 RTLO 10 9 8 7 6 5 4 3 2 1
❖
First Edition

This is the planet Earth a long, long time ago.

The planet is teeming with different forms of life, but the biggest and most dominant are the dinosaurs.

There were many different kinds of dinosaurs.

The sauropods were giant plant eaters
that walked on all fours.

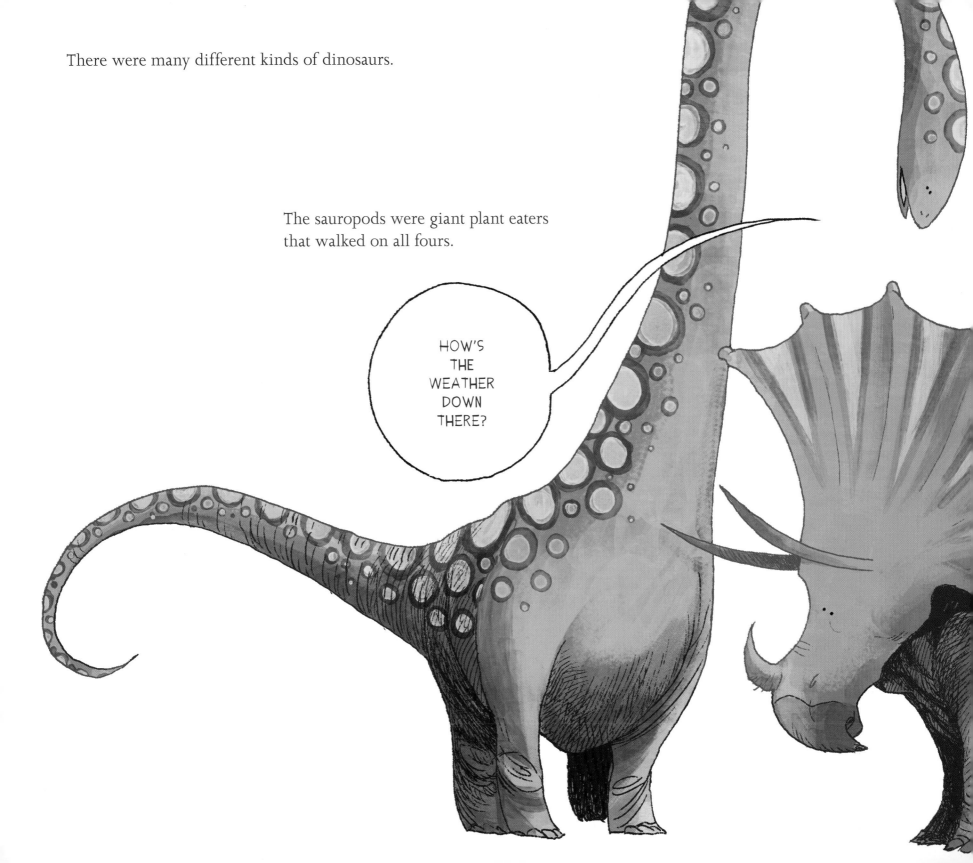

Don't forget the theropods. They came in all different sizes, but they all walked on two feet and loved to eat meat.

The ceratopsians weren't quite as large, but they had cool armored frills.

ARE YOU MEAT?

I COULD PUT MARSHMALLOWS ON MY HORNS, BUT THEY DON'T EXIST YET.

Everything was going along swimmingly until something appeared in the sky.

It was an asteroid.

It was very hot and very large and moving very fast.

9KM IN DIAMETER, ABOUT THE SIZE OF MOUNT EVEREST, AND MOVING 40,000 MILES PER HOUR

The asteroid hit the planet very hard, left a
very big hole, and made a very big mess.

There was ash and dust everywhere, enough to
coat the planet and block out the Sun.

Needless to say, it was a bad day for the dinosaurs
and just about anything else above ground.

More than 60 percent of all the plants and animals went extinct because of the asteroid and its aftermath. It was the end of the Cretaceous period and the age of the dinosaurs.

OR WAS IT?

Even under the most extreme circumstances, life tends to find a way. Scientists don't know exactly how or why certain animals survived after the asteroid hit. They do know that, in general, when there's a big disaster or environmental change, smaller, more adaptable animals are more likely to survive.

And sadly, over time, the big dinosaurs we all know so well from television and movies went extinct.

But while the big dinosaurs were no longer the planet's dominant form of life—mammals now hold that title—many dinosaurs survived. In fact, they went on to become one of Earth's most diverse groups of animals, with nearly 10,000 different species.

You know them better as birds.

That's right, **BIRDS ARE DINOSAURS!**

Don't believe me, ask this scientist . . .

Birds descended from a group of dinosaurs called "theropods" (those two-footed, meat-eating dinosaurs you remember from earlier).

Millions of years before the asteroid made such a big mess, theropods had begun to develop feathers as a way to keep warm. (Feathers are excellent insulation!) This process was part of their evolution.

Evolution is when a species changes over a long period of time to better fit their environment. Over millions of years, feathers continued to evolve until eventually the dinosaurs would be able to fly!

CROW

COELOPHYSIS

CONFUCIUSORNIS

CHIROSTENOTES

ARCHAEOPTERYX

GUANLONG

YI QI

OVIRAPTOR

Over the next few million years, birds spread their wings and moved into the environments that used to be home to their large dinosaur cousins.

In this new era we call the Cenozoic, birds would thrive and become one of the most diverse groups of animals on the planet!

THE CRETACEOUS

THE NEOGENE

Today, birds live on every continent and in every environment on Earth!

You've probably had dinosaur for dinner.

They no longer shake the Earth like their prehistoric ancestors, but these modern dinosaurs still make their presence felt everyday.

Dinosaurs help control our pests.

:crunch:
:crunch:

They clean up unpleasant messes.

They even pollinate our plants.

Who knew dinosaurs could be so helpful?

Modern dinosaurs and their prehistoric partners even share
some of the same behaviors, like . . .

nesting . . .

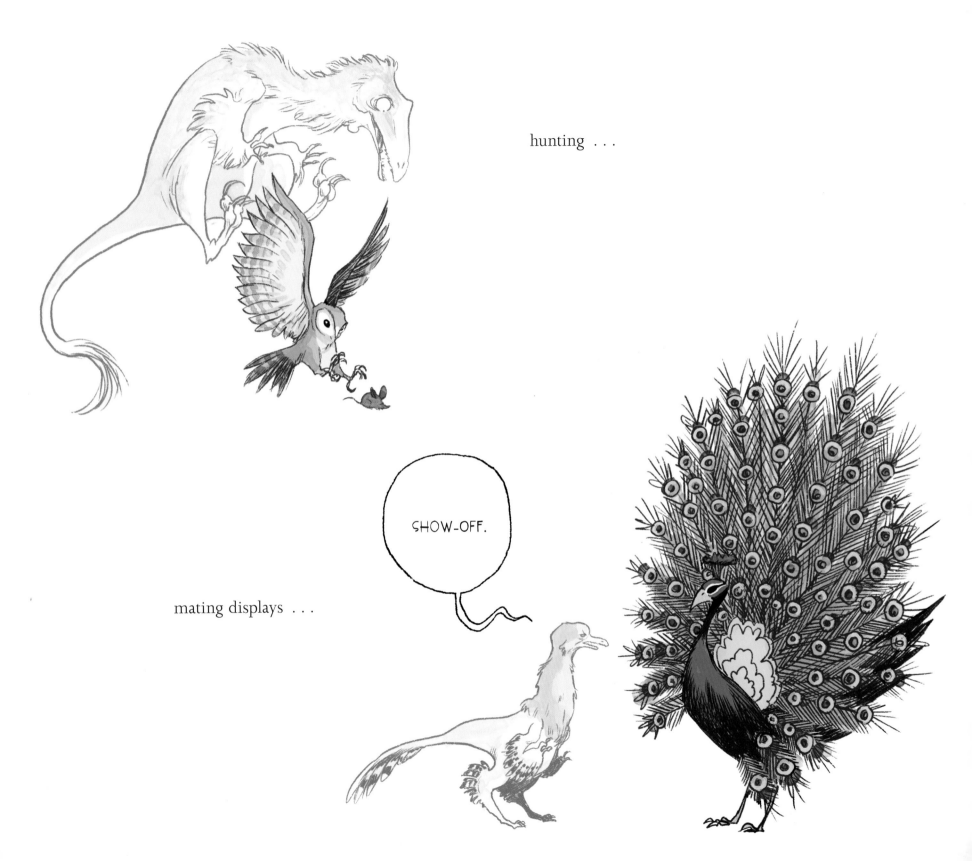

hunting . . .

mating displays . . .

SHOW-OFF.

. . . and migration.

Every time you hear a sparrow sing, every time
you hear a rooster crow, remember . . .

DINOSAURS ARE NOT EXTINCT!

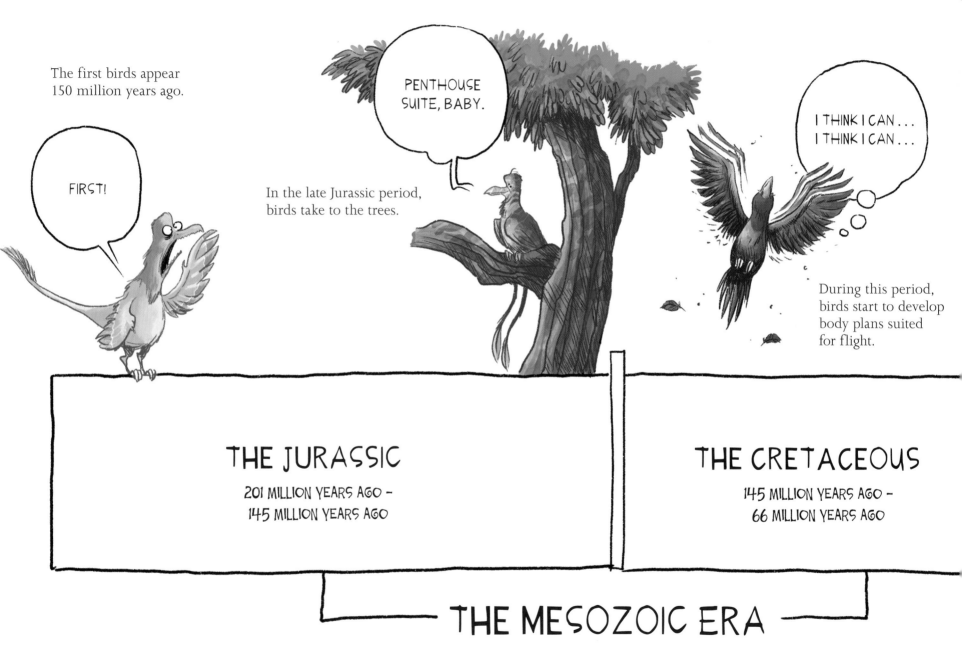

The first birds appear 150 million years ago.

In the late Jurassic period, birds take to the trees.

During this period, birds start to develop body plans suited for flight.

THE JURASSIC

201 MILLION YEARS AGO – 145 MILLION YEARS AGO

THE CRETACEOUS

145 MILLION YEARS AGO – 66 MILLION YEARS AGO

THE MESOZOIC ERA

AVIAN HISTORY

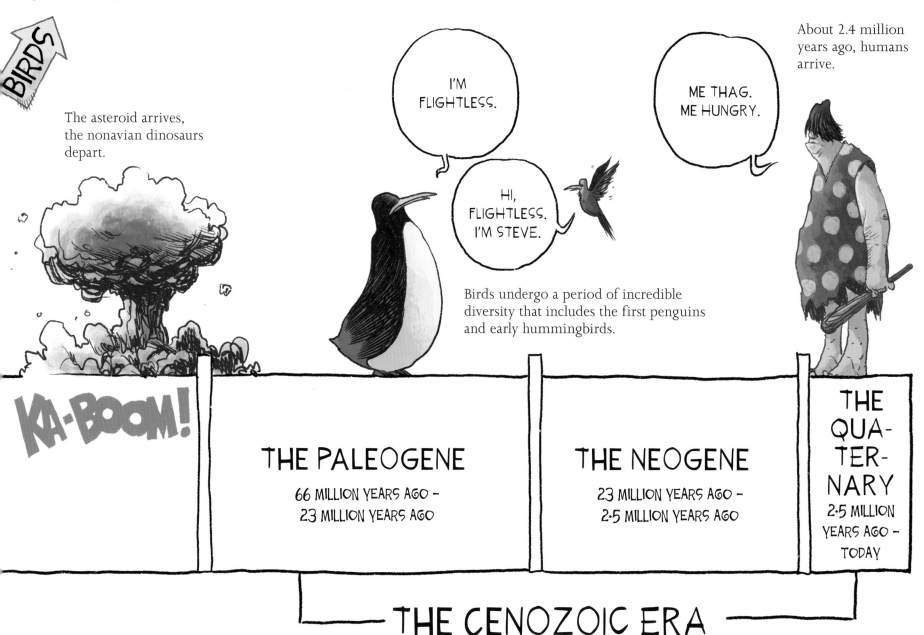

BIRDS

The asteroid arrives, the nonavian dinosaurs depart.

KA-BOOM!

I'M FLIGHTLESS.

HI, FLIGHTLESS. I'M STEVE.

Birds undergo a period of incredible diversity that includes the first penguins and early hummingbirds.

ME THAG. ME HUNGRY.

About 2.4 million years ago, humans arrive.

THE PALEOGENE
66 MILLION YEARS AGO –
23 MILLION YEARS AGO

THE NEOGENE
23 MILLION YEARS AGO –
2.5 MILLION YEARS AGO

THE QUA-TER-NARY
2.5 MILLION YEARS AGO –
TODAY

THE CENOZOIC ERA